LEGENDS OF WARFARE

AVIATION

Corsair

Vought's F4U in World War II and Korea

DAVID DOYLE

Schiffer Publishing Ltd

4880 Lower Valley Road • Atglen, PA 19310

Designed by Justin Watkinson
Type set in Impact/Minion Pro/Univers LT Std

ISBN: 978-0-7643-5503-5
Printed in China

Published by Schiffer Publishing, Ltd.
4880 Lower Valley Road
Atglen, PA 19310
Phone: (610) 593-1777; Fax: (610) 593-2002
E-mail: Info@schifferbooks.com
www.schifferbooks.com

For our complete selection of fine books on this and related subjects, please visit our website at www.schifferbooks.com. You may also write for a free catalog.

Schiffer Publishing's titles are available at special discounts for bulk purchases for sales promotions or premiums. Special editions, including personalized covers, corporate imprints, and excerpts, can be created in large quantities for special needs. For more information, contact the publisher.

We are always looking for people to write books on new and related subjects. If you have an idea for a book, please contact us at proposals@schifferbooks.com.

Acknowledgments

As with all of my projects, this book would not have been possible without the generous help of many friends. Instrumental to the completion of this book were Tom Kailbourn, Rich Kolasa, Dana Bell, Sean Hert, Scott Taylor, the staff and volunteers at the National Museum of Naval Aviation; Doug Siegfried with the Tailhook Association; and Robert Hanshew with the Naval History and Heritage Command. Most importantly, I am grateful for the help and support of my wonderful wife Denise.

COVER: Among the surviving airworthy Corsairs is Goodyear FG-1D Bureau Number (BuNo) 67089. It bears the nickname "Skyboss" with Yosemite Sam artwork and the fuselage code 555. Recently this Corsair was in the collection of the American Airpower Museum, Farmingdale, New York. *Rich Kolasa*

Contents

Introduction

Years before there was a Vought F4U Corsair, Chance Vought produced several other planes named Corsair for the US Navy, including the SBU-1 dive-bomber and the O2U scout and observation plane. Another distant precursor of the F4U was the Vought FU-1 fighter of the 1920s, an example of which is shown here. Not long before developing the F4U, Vought also produced for the Navy the OS2U Kingfisher observation float plane. *National Museum of Naval Aviation*

In early 1938, the US Navy was soliciting designs for a new carrier-based fighter. Proposals were requested for both single- and twin-engine designs. The single-engine design was to provide a range of at least 1,000 miles, a stall speed of seventy miles per hour or less, be armed with four machine guns (three with increased ammunition was an option), provisions to carry small underwing bombs, and provide maximum speed.

Vought responded with two proposals, both to be powered by air-cooled radial engines—one to be powered by the proven Pratt & Whitney R-1830 Twin Wasp, the other by the forthcoming XR-2800-2. Whereas at this time the Army Air Corps had a clear preference for liquid-cooled engines in fighters, which afforded better streamlining, at the cost of a vulnerable cooling system, the Navy opted for the air-cooled. While decidedly not aerodynamic, the air-cooled engine was less vulnerable to overheating and subsequent failure, important over the wide expanses of water, which limited forced landing and subsequent rescue possibilities.

In order to harness the power of the XR-2800-2, the designers turned to Hamilton Standard, who provided a thirteen-feet, four-inch, three-blade propeller. The massive propeller brought with it the problem of clearance—raising the prop far enough to not strike the ground/carrier deck. Fitting the aircraft with extra-long landing gear would raise the prop, but making the landing gear both long and strong enough to withstand the rigors of carrier operations was problematic. The solution was found in using an inverted gull wing, with the landing gear connecting at the low point. Added benefits of this design included improved pilot visibility and ditching characteristics.

In June 1938, the Navy contracted with Vought for a single prototype of the company's design V-166B, the XR-2800-powered proposal.

The XF4U-1 Corsair prototype and subsequent production models of the plane featured inverted gull wings, designed to minimize the length of the main landing-gear stuts. Given the large diameter of the propeller, very long struts would have been required if straight wings were used. Here, a gull-winged model of a Corsair is being used for wind-tunnel tests to collect data on its aerodynamic characteristics. Note the rounded nose, which was not a feature on the Corsairs.
National Archives and Records Administration

One prototype Corsair was constructed, Vought XF4U-1 Bureau Number (BuNo) 1443. Prominent on the leading edges of the center wing section are oblong openings containing intercooler-ventilation ducts and oil coolers. The plane was finished overall in Aluminum lacquer with Orange Yellow wing tops and leading edges. The bent wings necessitated three-part flaps on each side. *National Archives and Records Administration*

The new aircraft was given the government designation XF4U-1, and the Bureau of Aeronautics number (BuNo) assigned to it was 1443. As the engineering team led by Rex Beisel went about the detailed design, work began on a full-sized wooden mockup, which was complete and ready for Navy inspection on February 8, 1939.

With the mockup approved, work began on constructing the flyable prototype. The XF4U-1 first took to the air on May 29, 1940, with Lyman A. Bullard, Jr. at the controls. The flight progressed normally until an elevator trim tab failed, curtailing the flight, albeit with an uneventful landing.

On July 11, 1940, Vought test pilot Boone T. Guyton was taking the XF4U-1 on the aircraft's fifth flight when thirty-eight minutes into the flight both the weather began to turn bad and fuel began to run low. Guyton opted to set the aircraft down on the 14th fairway at Norwich Golf Club. Initially, the landing was uneventful, but the smooth, slick grass caused the fighter to slide rather than slow on brake application. The aircraft skidded across the fairway and into trees, flipping, crushing the tail and tearing the right wing off.

Foretelling the future of the type in combat, the pilot suffered only minor bumps and bruises, and the aircraft, though heavily damaged and requiring two months to repair, would fly again. During the repair the engine was moved slightly forward and the new propeller differed slightly from the original as well, having a broader tip.

Among those future flights, again with Guyton at the controls, was an October 1, 1940 flight from Stratford (Connecticut) to Hartford. On this flight the XF4U-1 had an average ground speed of 405 miles per hour, becoming the first single-engine US fighter to exceed 400 mph in level flight.

The series of flight tests revealed some deficiencies requiring correction. In some cases this was a change of design, but in other instances a change of specification was required. Such was the case when it was found that the required recovery from a two-turn spin was impossible without the use of an anti-spin chute.

The XF4U-1 is shown during construction on a stand with its landing gear extended. Some of the cowling panels have been removed. On the belly of the fuselage to the rear of the engine is a dark shape: this was an egg-shaped bomb-aiming window, through which the pilot sighted in order to release 5.2-pound antiaircraft bombs housed in bays on the bottom sides of the wings. These bombs were not carried on production Corsairs. *National Archives and Records Administration*

Other changes in specification were brought about by reports from Allied combat in Europe. Initially, the F4U-1 was to be armed with two .30-caliber machine guns in the cowl and two .50-caliber machine guns, one in each outer wing. Based on combat reports, this was determined to be insufficient, and the specification was subsequently rewritten.

Navy acceptance trials of the XF4U-1 began in February 1941, at Anacostia, Maryland. After acceptance, the XF4U-1 was used first as a platform for further refinement of the type before being sent to the Navy Technical Training Center in Norman, Oklahoma, and in December 1943, was deemed surplus and scrapped.

The XF4U-1 is shown in flight in an original color photograph. The apertures for a .50-caliber machine gun in each wing and the right .30-caliber machine-gun in the front of the cowling are visible. Note the orange finish on the gear-reduction housing on the front of the Pratt & Whitney XR-2800-4 radial engine: possibly Zinc Chromate primer with Iron Oxide mixed in. This was a primer coat sometimes seen on early Corsairs. Also worthy of notice are the manner in which the Orange Yellow paint wraps under the leading edge of the wing, and the way in which the Aluminum paint is applied to the bottom edge of the wing air scoops. *Stan Piet collection*

CHAPTER 2
F4U-1 "Birdcage" Corsair

The first production model of the Corsair was the Vought F4U-1. Shown in this and several following photos is the first F4U-1, BuNo 02153. The early F4U-1s had a two-color paint scheme: Blue Gray on the upper surfaces, the sides of the fuselage and vertical tail, and the bottoms of the outer wing sections; and Light Gray on the other lower surfaces. *National Archives and Records Administration*

Pleased with the results of flight tests of the XF4U-1, in April 1941, Vought was issued a contract for the construction of 625 F4U-1 aircraft. Preparations were immediately made to manufacture these aircraft, but the complexities of this process combined with the increasing demands placed on tooling suppliers resulted in the first production Corsair, Bureau Number 02153, not taking to the air until June 25, 1942, more than a year after the contract was issued.

The production F4U-1 differed considerably from the XF4U-1. While both had framed canopies—today referred to by enthusiasts as a "birdcage"—there were significant differences between the two canopies. The canopy of the production aircraft was moved thirty-two inches back along the fuselage and was slightly higher than that fitted to the prototype. The canopy itself was redesigned, with the pronounced angle of the trailing edge of the prototype canopy becoming much more subtle.

The relocation of the cockpit was the result of mounting a 237-gallon self-sealing main fuel tank directly behind the engine, whereas the prototype had two fuel tanks in the center wing section. Amor protection was added to the cockpit, along with bullet-resistant glass.

Further changes had to do with armament; the prototype's provision for a pair of cowl-mounted .30-caliber weapons and a pair of wing-mounted .50-caliber machine guns was eschewed in favor of three .50-caliber machine guns in each wing.

Interest from overseas buyers, coupled with the Navy's own demands, not only for the Corsair but also the OS2U Kingfisher, led to the government seeking alternate manufacturers for the Corsair.

In November 1941, a contract was placed with Brewster Aeronautical Corporation, and the following month a contract was issued to Goodyear Aircraft Corporation, Akron, Ohio.

The Brewster aircraft, designated the F3A-1, were assembled at Johnsville, Pennsylvania, utilizing major parts and sub-assemblies produced at the firm's Long Island City location, along with wing and tail components built by the company's Newark facility. The first sixty Corsairs built by Brewster featured the framed canopy.

The Goodyear-produced F4U-1 aircraft were designated FG-1. The Akron-based firm produced 299 aircraft with the so-called birdcage canopy.

F4U-1 BuNo 02153 is seen from the left side in a photograph dated July 15, 1942. The pitot tube was mounted on the leading edge of the left wing. On the forward part of the wingtip was a clear lens for the red-colored left navigation light; the bulb on the right wing was green. Aft of the cockpit canopy on each side of the fuselage was a semi-elliptical window, sometimes called a tunnel window, to allow the pilot some visibility to the rear. *National Archives and Records Administration*

In a rear view of F4U-1 02153, note that early on the doors for the tail landing gear did not have cutouts on their inboard sides, since the shorter, early landing gear was able to retract completely into its bay. Early-production F4U-1s such as this one had a 29.25-inch antenna mast fabricated from phenolic plastic. These masts tended to break off during flight because of harmonic vibrations, so shortened masts or masts made of other materials were introduced. The vertical fin and rudder were inclined two degrees to the left to counteract propeller torque. *National Archives and Records Administration*

The original short tail landing gear of the F4U-1 is visible from this angle on BuNo 02153. The hook end of the retracted arrestor hook is visible at the rear of the tail landing gear bay. The horizontal stabilizers and the vertical fin were of aluminum-frame-and-skin construction, while the elevators and the rudder were formed of fabric over aluminum frames. The rudder had one trim tab, while each elevator had one trim tab and one balance tab. *National Archives and Records Administration*

As seen on F4U-1 BuNo 02153, initially the Corsairs had three stripes on the propeller tips: from outboard to inboard they were red, yellow, and blue; the blue is not readily visible in this photograph, possibly because sometimes the propeller blades of early F4U-1s exclusive of the tips were painted Insignia Blue on the front and rear. Later, the prop tips were painted yellow. Each of the outer folding wing sections housed in its forward end a sixty-three-gallon fuel tank. The skin of the wings enclosing those tanks was aluminum. The remainder of the outer-wing surfaces were covered with fabric. There also was a 237-gallon fuel tank in the fuselage forward of the cockpit. *National Archives and Records Administration*

A view of the underside of an early F4U-1 in flight illustrates the practice of painting the bottoms of the outer wing sections Blue Gray, while the remainder of the undersides of the plane were Light Gray. Painting the bottoms of the outer wing sections in this manner made them less visible than if they were Light Gray when the wings were folded while the planes were spotted on the flight deck of an aircraft carrier. The egg-shaped bomb-aiming window of the XF4U-1 had been replaced by nearly square windows, as seen here. *National Archives and Records Administration*

An F4U-1 cockpit is viewed from the left side in a June 1942 photograph. Above the instrument panel are crash pads, between which is an early-model Mk.8 illuminated gun sight. At the lower right is the pilot's seat, to the front of which is his control stick. The F4U-1 lacked a floor in the cockpit. Instead, there were metal troughs below the rudder pedals to support the pilot's feet. The right rudder pedal and foot trough is to the right of the control stick. The reason for the lack of the floor was so the pilot could look down through the bomb-aiming window in the belly of the fuselage. *National Archives and Records Administration*

VS-5468 F4U-1 PILOT'S COCKPIT-3/4 RIGHT HAND 6-12-42

Details of the right side of an early-production F4U-1 cockpit are shown. At the front end of the console are three control levers for the cooling flaps, to the right of which are a keying switch and controls for the recognition lights. The bulk of the console was occupied by switches and circuit breakers for various electrical systems. The quadrant to the rear of the console is the arrestor-hook control. The cylindrical object adjacent to the front of the sliding-canopy opening is a light. On the right wall of the cockpit are radio controls. *National Archives and Records Administration*

The left side of an early F4U-1 cockpit is shown. The engine-control unit, or throttle quadrant, is on the side wall above the console. On the console are electrical switches, the fuel-selector switch, and trim-tab controls. The quadrant to the rear of the console is the wing-folding control. The handle with the knurled grip to the left of the pilot's seat was part of the hand pump for the emergency powering of the hydraulic system. *National Archives and Records Administration*

F4U-1 Corsairs are under construction at the Chance Vought factory at Stratford, Connecticut, on August 12, 1942. On the plane in the foreground, cowling panels are absent, allowing a look at the Pratt & Whitney R-2800-8 radial engine. The part of the leading edge of the right wing that includes the air scoop has been removed, showing the forward part of the wing root. At this point in time, Vought had not come fully up to speed in F4U-1 production. The Navy accepted only nine F4U-1s during that month. *National Archives and Records Administration*

The same F4U-1 seen in the preceding photo is viewed from a different perspective on the Vought assembly line on August 12, 1942. Directly above the head of the man standing in the space where the air scoop will be mounted in the leading edge of the center section of the wing is a rectangular opening with a temporary cover on it; this was the outer face of the right-hand intercooler. The round opening in the wing root to the front of the intercooler is the lower part of the air duct leading to the supercharger. *National Archives and Records Administration*

The Vought final-assembly line was where subassemblies were joined together into finished aircraft. In this December 23, 1942 photo, in the foreground are F4U-1 fuselages with the empennages and center wing sections installed, but outer wings and power plants are not yet attached. Starting with the third plane in that line are airframes with the outer wings installed. On the next line to the right are dozens of subassemblies comprising the cockpit section of the fuselage mated to the center wing section. Farther to the rear are various fuselage and empennage subassemblies. *National Archives and Records Administration*

In an August 12, 1942 photograph of the Vought production line, three F4U-1s with more or less complete fuselages are undergoing final assembly in the foreground, while in the background are a number of wing center sections and various fuselage sections. The third plane in the row does not yet have its outer wing sections installed. On the second Corsair, national insignia have been applied to the wings, and a jury strut, or detachable brace, is attached to the right outer wing section to the fuselage to hold the wing in a stationary vertical attitude. *National Archives and Records Administration*

In the four months following the preceding August 1942 photographs, production of F4U-1s steadily increased, as is apparent in this photograph of a very full assembly line at the Vought factory on December 23, 1942. Whereas the Navy accepted only nine F4U-1s in August, by December the Navy accepted sixty-eight of the planes, with total acceptances of 178 Corsairs that year. During the following year, the Navy would accept ten times that number of Corsairs: 1,785. On the left are F4U-1s undergoing final assembly, while on the right are subassemblies with the center section of the wing and the cockpit section of the fuselage. *National Museum of Naval Aviation*

The final-assembly line at the Vought factory at Stratford, Connecticut, is viewed from the front on December 23, 1942. More than a dozen airframes are on this line. Note the variation in the shades of paint on such components as the rudders and the canopy frames, compared to the paint on the fuselages. By now, the propellers were finished in black, with yellow tips. On all but the closest Corsair, jury struts are attached to the fuselages, for securing the outer wing sections in an upright position when necessary. *National Museum of Naval Aviation*

This final view of the final-assembly line at Vought on December 23, 1943 shows F4U-1s from the left rear. On the left wings of the first three planes, the main access doors for the machine-gun and ammunition bays are installed and are closed, but the rear panels for the machine-gun bays are not installed. On the fuselages below the vertical fins are hinged access doors in the open position. Stored in an upright position in the center background are outer wing sections. *National Museum of Naval Aviation*

A pilot adjusts his parachute pack preparatory to a test flight in an F4U-1 Corsair at Vought's factory in Stratford, Connecticut, in 1942. The demarcations between the upper, Blue Gray, and lower, Light Gray, camouflage paint are readily visible. The colors had a feathered edge between them. Note that the black propeller blades lack yellow tips on their rear facets. *National Museum of Naval Aviation*

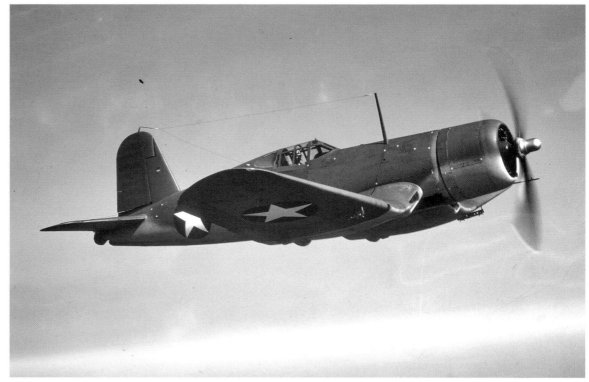

An F4U-1 is undergoing a test flight. This is an early-production example with the shorter tail landing gear with no cutouts in the gear doors to accommodate the wheel. The small white dots at various places on the fuselage are inspection stickers. Visible below each of the outer wing sections is a detachable rack for a 100-pound bomb. *National Museum of Naval Aviation*

This early-production F4U-1 features what appears to be an early application of a tricolor camouflage scheme on a Corsair. This scheme, introduced on January 5, 1943, featured Sea Blue on upper surfaces, White on lower surfaces, and Intermediate Blue on the vertical tail, the sides of the fuselage, and the bottoms of the outer wing sections. The small, white object to the rear of the tunnel window is an insulator for a wire-antenna lead-in. On the right elevator, note that the balance tab is raised at a higher angle than the larger trim tab on the elevator tab's inboard side. Note how the arrestor hook was attached to the tail-gear strut.

A pilot goes over his checklist preparatory to a flight in an F4U-1. Many fine details are available in this photo, from the Hamilton Standard propeller, with a diameter of thirteen feet, four inches, to the front of the R-2800-8 engine, the cowling and cowl flaps, and the main landing gear. On the underside of the center wing section aft of the leading-edge air scoops are the oil-cooler doors in the open position. Between those doors is the intercooler flap in the lowered position.

Although Vought was the principal producer of birdcage Corsairs, Goodyear Aircraft Corportion also manufactured a version designated the FG-1, with total production of 299 aircraft. The assembly line was at Akron, Ohio. On this example painted in tricolor camouflage, note the tape over the machine-gun ports on the leading edges of the wings and the cartridge-ejector chutes on the bottom of the wing.

Mechanics are servicing several Goodyear FG-1 birdcage Corsairs. On the closest plane, heavy streaking from engine oil is visible on the underside of the center wing section. With the cowling panels removed from the engine-accessory compartments in the nearest two planes, visible at the front is the intermediate intercooler duct.

Workers are operating on an FG-1 on the Goodyear Aircraft final-assembly line. Note the round access holes on the vertical tail: two on the vertical fin and one on the rudder. On the side of the turtledeck to the right of the woman standing on the center section of the wing is the semi-elliptical shape of the left tunnel window; it is covered with protective paper and masking tape.

The following series of photos of FG-1 Corsairs under construction was taken at the Goodyear Aircraft factory in Akron, Ohio. Seen here is a row of R-2800-8 engine assemblies with the nose-cowl assemblies installed. In the right background are several fuselage and center-wing subassemblies. In the far left background is the final-assembly area, with several complete or nearly-complete FG-1s in view.

In a head-on view of a Goodyear FG-1 nearing completion, the wings are raised to the vertical, steadied by jury struts attached to the fuselage. The lower lips of the air scoops on the leading edge of the center wing section are not yet installed. The machine-gun-bay doors are open; above those doors, the rectangular-shaped gap-cover doors for the ammunition bays also are open. The outer-wing flaps are lowered.

An FG-1 undergoing final assembly is viewed from above on the Goodyear assembly line. On the bottom of the right outer wing panel are three round identification lights. The front one was red, the middle one was dark blue (or green when illuminated), and the rear one amber. The rear of the fuselage is supported by a pipe inserted through the hoist holes forward of the vertical fin; a jack on each side of the fuselage holds up the pipe and the plane.

Mechanics hoist a Hamilton Standard three-bladed propeller onto the propeller shaft of the engine of an FG-1. The hoist chain is attached to a fitting clamped to one of the propeller blades. These propellers had a diameter of thirteen feet, four inches. The oval-shaped Hamilton Standard logo decals are on the prop blades.

Workers are going about their tasks on a Goodyear FG-1. A trolley is supporting the plane underneath the center wing section. The main landing gear is in a partially retracted position. The main-gear units retracted to the rear and also rotated sideways, as seen here, so that the wheels would fit into the shallow landing-gear bays. Protective paper has been taped over the leading edges of the outer wings, apparently to keep foreign objects out of the machine-gun apertures.

A group of FG-1s undergoing final assembly are seen on the floor of the Goodyear Aircraft plant at Akron, Ohio. An unusually clear view of the underside of a right outer-wing section is available in the foreground. On the second plane, the gap-filler plate between the inboard and center flaps on the right wing is visible. Although the sliding canopies of these planes are covered with protective paper, their tops have the distinctive downward slope to the rear of the birdcage canopy, rather than the semi-bubble canopy.

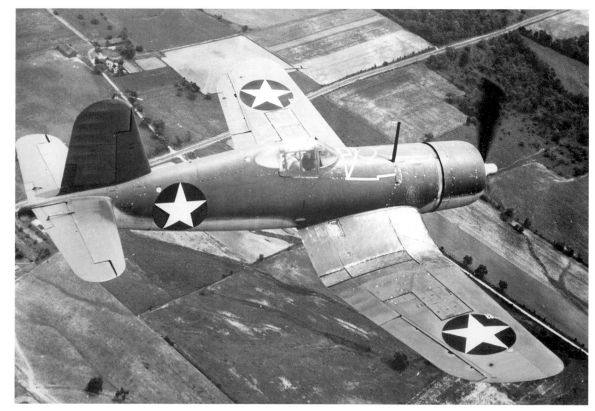

A Brewster-built F3A1 Corsair flies over countryside at relatively low altitude. It has neatly-applied white tape over the joints on the fuselage forward of the cockpit, below and to the rear of the fuel filler, to prevent fuel from seeping into the joints. The white dot adjacent to the upper left edge of the national insignia on the fuselage was a plug for the openings for a hoist bar.

CHAPTER 3
F4U-2

Even before the first F4U-1 had rolled off Vought's Stratford, Connecticut, assembly line, the Navy was expressing interest in a night fighter version of the aircraft. Radar, which was then in its infancy, was to be the key component of the new aircraft, which was to be designated F4U-2.

The initial Navy contract for the F4U-2 was for a meager fifteen aircraft. Rather than disrupt F4U-1 production for these few aircraft, the decision was made to create the -2 by modifying aircraft completed as -1s. The first production F4U-1, BuNo 02153, was modified to be the F4U-2 prototype. The aircraft were flown to the Naval Aircraft Factory in Philadelphia beginning in September 1942, and the first conversion was completed on January 4, 1943.

Externally, the F4U-2 could be distinguished from the -1 by the bulbous radome on the leading edge of the right wing. The dome held the antenna for the AIA radar set. To maintain balance of the aircraft, the outboard gun of the same wing was deleted. Also readily visible were the extended flame dampeners on the engine exhaust stubs. This served to both decrease the visibility of the aircraft in night skies, and to improve night vision on the part of the Corsair pilot.

Beneath the aircraft were visible the antennas for the AN/APN-1 radar altimeter, resembling inverted Ts.

Because of the critical shortage of the AIA radar sets, many F4U-2s were shipped to their assigned units without the radar being installed. Despite this, the number of aircraft on order eventually climbed to thirty-two, although one of these, BuNo 02682, was actually never fitted with radar at all. Many of those that were completed had their radar sets installed in the field by squadron maintenance men.

Given the experience of field maintenance teams installing the radar equipment, it is not surprising that the technicians of VMF(N)-532 on Roi installed the F4U-2 equipment in two raised canopy (F4U-1A) aircraft in 1944, creating their own variation.

The F4U-2 night-fighters were a conversion of the F4U-1, featuring a radome on the right wing containing an AIA radar antenna as well as other modifications. The outboard right machine gun was deleted to compensate for the weight of the radar installation, a small radar scope was installed on the instrument panel, and radio-altimeter and radar-beacon-transponder sets were installed. A total of thirty-three F4U-1s were converted to F4U-2s: thirty-one at the Naval Aircraft Factory in Philadelphia, and two in the field in the Marshall Islands. Here, an F4U-2 assigned to VF(N)-101 is being brought up on an elevator on USS *Enterprise* (CV-6) in preparation for a mission on January 20, 1944. *National Museum of Naval Aviation*

Three F4U-2s of VF(N)-101 are running up their engines prior to takeoff from USS *Enterprise* on February 16, 1944. The mission for the day was a raid against Japanese forces in Truk Atoll. On the belly of the nearest Corsair, below the national insignia, is a radio-altimeter antenna, shaped like an inverted T. This was part of the standard F4U-2 conversion. Note the arrangement of two machine guns in the right wing and three in the left wing. *National Museum of Naval Aviation*

An F4U-2 is preparing for takeoff on USS *Enterprise*. The number 8 is marked on both of the main landing gear doors, and a number 8 is faintly visible to the front of the national insignia on the fuselage. Also in view are the flame-dampening exhausts extending from the lower rear of the cowl, a feature of the F4U-2 to reduce its visibility at night. *Navy History and Heritage Command*

The pilot of an F4U-2 night-fighter numbered 10 on the main-gear doors is intently watching the launch officer and will begin his takeoff roll as soon as the officer lowers the flag in his right hand. The two sets of flame-dampening exhausts are visible just aft of the bottom of the cowl. The plane was assigned to VF(N)-101 and the scene was on USS *Enterprise* on April 30, 1944. *National Museum of Naval Aviation*

Another night-fighting squadron to make use of the F4U-2 was VMF(N)-532. One of that unit's F4U-2s is preparing for takeoff on the flight deck of USS *Windham Bay* (CVE-92) on July 12, 1944, while other F4U-2s snaked around the aft end of the flight deck await their turn. VMF(N)-532 was the sole USMC squadron to be equipped with F4U-2s. Number 208 is in the left foreground, while number 205 is preparing for takeoff to the right. *National Museum of Naval Aviation*

Two F4U-2 night-fighting Corsairs from VF(N)-101 are being prepared for launching from USS *Enterprise* prior to a raid on Truk in February 1944. The forward Corsair has the number 9 on its main-gear doors, while the one to the rear is numbered 11. These two planes were among the Birdcage Corsairs that were modified to immobilize or eliminate the two top cowl flaps, to alleviate the problem of leaking oil spattering the windscreen. F4U-2s of VF(N)-101 had tricolor camouflage schemes, except with Black paint replacing Intermediate Blue on the sides of the fuselage. *National Museum of Naval Aviation*

F4U-2 fuselage number 201, nicknamed "Shirley June," was flown by Maj. Everett H. Vaughan of VMF(N)-532. Maj. Vaughan is shown in his plane at Kwajalein Atoll around 1944. "Shirley June" was painted in block letters on the forward fuselage, while "Maj. E.H. Vaughan" was painted in script on the fuselage below the sliding canopy. The sliding canopy was the late-production model with a bulge on the top forward clear panel to accommodate a rear-view mirror, as the installation of the pilot's Brownscope rear-view periscope, originally mounted at the top of the windscreen, had been discontinued. *National Museum of Naval Aviation*

CHAPTER 4
F4U-1A: The First Raised Canopy Corsair

While the F4U-1 was certainly a formidable fighter aircraft, limitations of the pilot's field of vision, both from the long nose ahead of him and the canopy frames around him, detracted from the Corsair's combat fitness. The Navy Bureau of Aeronautics directed that Vought raise the pilot to improve his vision, with the intent being that the changes would be made to production going forward, and also to retrofit existing aircraft.

F4U-1 Bureau Number 02557 was modified to serve as the prototype of the raised cabin concept and was completed in February 1943. The redesigned canopy had significantly fewer metal framing members obstructing the view and also provided greater headroom. Even more significantly, the installation of the pilot's seat was modified, even though the seat itself remained the same, such that it was mounted further forward and at a more upright angle, and could be raised an additional three inches. All of these changes were made to improve visibility.

While today the improved aircraft is widely known as the F4U-1A, no Navy documents will be found with this nomenclature, because in March 1943, the Bureau of Aeronautics refused Vought's request to use this nomenclature for the revised aircraft. Part of the Bureau's reasoning stemmed from their intent at that time to bring all the older aircraft up to the new standard, thus making the distinction irrelevant. Vought, Brewster, and Goodyear were allowed to use the -1A designator internally, but officially it was the raised cabin or cockpit aircraft, while the initial aircraft were "low cockpit model" or "early production."

Ultimately, the complexity and associated expense that would be involved in retrofitting the raised cockpit to existing aircraft forced such plans to be cancelled.

Shortly after the introduction of the raised canopy into Corsair production, the tail wheel strut was lengthened, forcing the nose down, thereby improving visibility when landing. The type was further improved through the installation of a Brewster-designed, 1,000-pound capacity centerline bomb rack beginning with Vought F4U-1A Bureau Number 17930 and Goodyear FG-1 Bureau Number 13572. Alternatively, the centerline stores station could be used to carry a 170-gallon capacity drop tank.

A critical shortcoming of the F4U-1 was its low cockpit and canopy as well as the frame of the canopy, which conspired to limit pilot visibility. Thus, in 1943, Vought commenced Engineering Project 108: a group of modifications to provide the pilot with better visibility, chief of which were the replacement of the birdcage canopy with a newly designed, semi-bubble canopy, and a more vertical pilot's seat that could be raised three inches higher than the seat of the F4U-1. Despite Vought's recommendation that the revised plane be designated the F4U-1A, the Navy insisted on referring to it as the F4U-1 Raised Cabin Version (or Raised Cockpit Version). Vought stuck with the F4U-1A designation, and for purposes of this book, the plane will be referred to as the F4U-1A. This example, photographed in 1944, has the higher tail landing gear introduced partway through F4U-1A production.
National Archives and Records Administration

A specimen of the semi-bubble canopy installed on the F4U-1As is viewed from the right side. These canopies provided much better visibility for the pilot than the framed canopy of the F4U-1. However, the semi-bubble canopies had two rather thick longitudinal frames on the upper parts of the units, somewhat hindering visibility. The curved, painted panel at the upper rear of the canopy was armor. *National Archives and Records Administration*

A factory-fresh Vought F4U-1A is seen from the left rear. On the rudder is the actuator for the rudder trim tab. Faintly visible is a cutout in the left tail-gear door to provide clearance for the tail wheel, which could not be retracted entirely into the gear bay because of the lengthened landing-gear strut. Aft of the cockpit is a VHF mast antenna. *National Archives and Records Administration*

The same F4U-1A is observed from the right rear with its flaps lowered. The actuator for the trim tab on the right elevator was on the top side, while the actuator for the left elevator's trim tab was on the bottom. *National Archives and Records Administration*

The propeller on this F4U-1A was the early-style Hamilton Standard model with a thin chord near the propeller hub. Later, a Hamilton Standard prop with a wider chord near the hub would be substituted. The interiors of the main landing gear doors are painted the same white color as the underside of the plane. *National Archives and Records Administration*

A trio of Vought F4U-1As are being subjected to their acceptance flights around late 1943 or early 1944. An acceptance flight was a general test of the proper functioning of an aircraft's systems by one of the manufacturer's test pilots. *National Museum of Naval Aviation*

F4U-1 BuNo 17930 was noteworthy for introducing several new features to the model: stall warning, a thirty-two-inch aluminum antenna mast, a combination landing-gear and dive-brake lever, and a rudder-trough superstructure. Note the short actuating arm for the left balance tab on the elevator, and the long actuating arm for the trim tab on the right elevator. The order of the long and short actuating arms was reversed on the undersides of the elevators. *Navy History and Heritage Command*

This flightline consists of Goodyear-produced FG-1As, counterparts to the F4U-1A, with early-style semi-bubble canopies with the two upper fore-and-aft frame members. The plane in the left foreground has the tricolor camouflage paint scheme, and as far as can be determined, the other Corsairs in the photo are similarly painted.

Brewster Aeronautical Corporation produced a version of the F4U-1A, designated the F3A-1A. This USMC example, BuNo 11289, was painted overall in the Glossy Sea Blue scheme introduced in 1945. It bears group commander's markings and the markings by the cockpit of Lt. Col. Joseph N. Renner, of the 1st Marine Aircraft Wing. There are at least two kill markings on the fuselage in the form of small Japanese flags. A 170-gallon Duramold auxiliary fuel tank is mounted on the centerline of the fuselage. The marking H-75 is on the fuselage and under the left wing. *National Museum of Naval Aviation*

An "FT" for Flight Test marking is on the cowling of Brewster F3A-1 BuNo 04591 at the Naval Air Test Center, NAS Patuxent River, Maryland, on March 15, 1944. This Corsair is painted in USN tricolor camouflage. Some of the skin joints forward of the windscreen have been covered with white tape. *National Archives and Records Administration*

The Royal Navy acquired a version of the Brewster F3A-1A for the Fleet Air Arm, designating the aircraft the Corsair Mk.III. This example, painted in British camouflage and markings, was photographed at the Naval Air Test Center (NATC) at Naval Air Station Patuxent River, Maryland. Painted on the cowling is the code "FT" and a nickname, "Moe." There were no wingtip navigation lights or machine guns on this plane. *National Museum of Naval Aviation*

Alphabetically, the next model of Corsair produced was the F4U-1C. While the first 20 mm-armed F4U, Bureau Number 50277, was based on the birdcage Corsair, and was completed in August 1943, the next 200 were built between July and November 1944, and were nearly identical to the F4U-1D (described in chapter 4). All of these aircraft were built by Vought, and their production coincided with production of the F4U-1D.

The objective of the 20 mm armament was to provide a heavier-hitting round with greater mass than afforded by even the fabled .50-caliber machine gun. The F4U-1C was armed with four AN/M2 cannons, which were license-built variations of the Hispano-Suiza HS.404 autocannon. These guns had a rate of fire of 600 to 700 rounds per minute, and the 20 mm ball round had a projectile weight of .28 pounds (1,960 grains), with a muzzle velocity of 2,850 feet per second. By comparison, the .50-caliber round weighed about 700 grains and had a muzzle velocity of 2,810 feet per second,

with a rate of fire of about 800 rounds per minute. Thus, a three-second burst from the F4U-1C put 39.2 pounds of projectile on target, whereas the six .50-caliber machine gun version delivered a little more than half that much weight, 24 pounds.

Unfortunately, ammunition stowage for the 20 mm rounds was problematic, with the F4U-1C hoisting aloft 924 rounds, whereas its .50-caliber armed brethren carried 2,400 rounds of machine gun ammo.

The move toward armament heavier than .50-caliber was not unique to the F4U-1C. The Navy pushed heavily for 20 mm armament for several aircraft (as well, of course, as for shipboard antiaircraft service), while the Army advanced development of a .60-caliber machine gun. Despite the Chief of Naval Operations pushing for 20 mm armament for future fighter development, forty-seven of the F4U-1Cs were refitted with six .50-caliber machine guns.

Although one might assume that, because of its -1C suffix, the Vought F4U-1C preceded the F4U-1D, this aircraft actually was based on the F4U-1D airframe, not the F4U-1A airframe. The F4U-1C substituted four 20 mm Hispano M2 cannons for the typical six .50-caliber machine guns of the Corsairs. Two hundred examples were completed. This one marked with the number 277 on the cowling was photographed during 1944. *National Museum of Naval Aviation*

The barrels of the 20 mm cannons of the F4U-1C protruded through metal fairings that were attached to the leading edges of the wings. Caps are fitted over the muzzles on this example to keep out dust and moisture. The propeller was the shorter-diameter (thirteen feet, one inch) Hamilton Standard Hydromatic type used on the F4U-1D and featured a wider chord near the propeller hub. *National Museum of Naval Aviation*

A F4U-1C wing is depicted, showing the aft door of the cannon bay removed, exposing the receivers of the two 20 mm cannons to view. Details of the wing panels and the framework that will be covered with fabric are available. To the right are the folded access doors of the cannon bay. The dark spot on the forward, metal-clad part of the outer wing is the opening for the fuel filler for the left leading-edge tank. *National Archives and Records Administration*

The 20 mm Hispano M2 cannons in the wings of the F4U-1C were staggered, with the outboard guns farther aft than the inboard ones. The complement of ammunition for the four cannons was 924 rounds, or 261 rounds per gun. *National Museum of Naval Aviation*

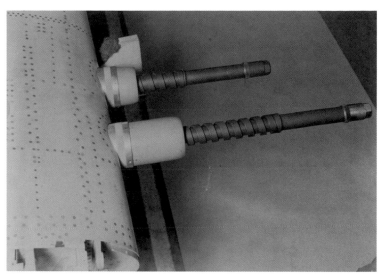

The barrels of the two 20 mm cannons in the left wing of an F4U-1C are shown. The tubular metal fairings through which the barrels protruded had rounded leading edges, and these fittings were removable. *National Archives and Records Administration*

The underside of the right wing of an F4U-1C under construction is depicted. To the left are the gun fairings and the rectangular openings for the spent-casing ejector chutes. To the right are the frames for the three identification lights. Fabric skin has yet to be installed over the bare framework to the right. *National Archives and Records Administration*

Cannon-bay access doors have been opened (right) to expose the 20 mm ammunition feeds in the left wing of an F4U-1C. The front of the wing is to the right. The aft door of the cannon bay is in the closed position. *National Archives and Records Administration*

CHAPTER 6
F4U-1D

Although the centerline stores pylon introduced during production of the F4U-1A was of considerable benefit, the Bureau of Aeronautics desired even more external stores capability. By late 1943, efforts were underway to fit the Corsair with two pylons on the wing center section.

While initial efforts focused on only one pylon including provisions for a drop tank, by March 1944, it was decided that both pylons, which by then had been in production for a couple of months, be equipped for drop tanks. The first 290 to leave the assembly line with two pylons were initially equipped for the drop tank on the right pylon only until June 1944. At that time the Bureau of Aeronautics ordered that these aircraft be retrofitted to allow use of drop tanks from both pylons. At the same time the classification of F4U-1D was initiated.

After the first 290 twin-pylon Corsairs had been completed by Vought, the Bureau of Aeronautics decided that Vought aircraft with two pylons would be classified as F4U-1D. Goodyear-built examples were classified as FG-1D. Owing to management and labor difficulties, the Navy halted Brewster production of the Corsair prior to the introduction of the twin-pylon model.

Initial twin-pylon Corsairs retained the provision for centerline external stores as well, however that feature was later abandoned as being made redundant by the new twin-pylon configuration.

During the course of F4U-1D production several other detail changes were made, including the change from a 13′4″ propeller to a 13′1″ propeller at Bureau Number 57356, and the addition of racks for four five-inch rockets under each wing at Bureau Number 82253. With Vought production of the F4U-1D totaling 1,685 and Goodyear's production of the comparable FG-1D equaling 1,997, the -1D was the most common Corsair variant to see combat in World War II.

The F4U-1D marked the coming-of-age of the Corsair as a fighter-bomber. Previously, Corsairs had been equipped initially to carry two 100-pound bombs on wing pylons, and later they had the capability to haul up to a 1,000-pound bomb on the Brewster belly rack. With the F4U-1D, two factory-installed pylons were installed under the center wing section, each of which was capable of carrying up to a 1,000-pound bomb or a 154-gallon auxiliary fuel tank. Early examples of the F4U-1D, such as this one, were painted in the tricolor camouflage scheme. *National Museum of Naval Aviation*

The Fleet Air Arm of the Royal Navy operated Goodyear FG-1As and FG-1Ds (comparable to the F4U-1A and F4U-1D) under the name Corsair Mk.IV. This Corsair Mk.IV bore Royal Navy serial number KD 365 to the front of the horizontal stabilizer. The photo was dated September 23, 1944.

Starting with BuNo 57583, the two longitudinal frame members on the upper part of the semi-bubble canopy of the F4U-1D were eliminated, resulting in much better visibility for the pilot. The canopy is partially open in this photo taken in early 1944. Visible through the sliding canopy is the pilot's headrest. *National Archives and Records Administration*

A frameless canopy for an F4U-1D is seen from the right rear. On the interior of the canopy frame, toward the bottom on each side is a canopy-release handle. On the upper part of the front frame of the canopy are three rear-view mirrors. *National Archives and Records Administration*

The following series of photos documents the wing pylons as mounted on F4U-1Ds. Early-production F4U-1Ds were equipped to carry centerline auxiliary fuel tanks or bombs with electrical releases, in addition to the two standard pylons. Later F4U-1Ds lacked fuel lines at the centerline hardpoints and substituted manual bomb-release mechanisms at those hardpoints. Still later, in 1945, fuel lines and electrical releases were restored to the centerline hardpoints. *National Archives and Records Administration*

A Corsair is shown with only one pylon installed, under the right wing, on December 27, 1943. An auxiliary fuel tank is mounted on the pylon. Early in the operational service of the F4U-1D, the official practice in the Navy was to mount a bomb on each pylon, but auxiliary fuel tanks were restricted to the right pylon. Starting in March 1944, fuel tanks were authorized for both pylons. *National Archives and Records Administration*

In a companion piece to the preceding photo, a worker is cranking the manual bomb hoist up to the shackles that will secure the bomb to the pylon. The hoist cable is attached to a sling around the bomb. Panels are removed from the underside of the engine-accessory compartment at the upper center. The right pylon has its fairing installed. The presence of a bomb-aiming window on the belly of the plane indicates that it likely was an F4U-1A being used as a test bed for the pylons; this window was discontinued during F4U-1A production. *National Archives and Records Administration*

The pylons on the F4U-1Ds had streamlined fairings around the bomb or drop-tank rack. This photo dated December 20, 1943, shows the fairing removed from the left pylon. The tube to the lower left that is attached to the bomb rack is the upper part of a manually operated bomb hoist. At the bottom of the photo is the top of a bomb being lifted by the hoist cable up to the shackles. *National Archives and Records Administration*

A combination of bombs and an auxiliary fuel tank are mounted on this Corsair. The tank was the Duramold model with a capacity of approximately 160 gallons. Duramold is a composite material composed of thin strips of birch impregnated with phenolic resin and laminated under heat and pressure, forming a durable, lightweight material. The tank was attached to the aircraft by fin-like extensions built into the top of the tank. *National Archives and Records Administration*

One of the surviving, airworthy Goodyear F4U-1Ds, BuNo 92471, comes in for a landing. This plane currently is nicknamed "Marine's Dream" and bears civil registration number N773RD. It bears a replica of the national insignia with the white side bars and red border that was briefly in use from June to September 1943. *Rich Kolasa*

Two restored Corsairs are on display at an air show. A few details of the wingfold joint on the closer plane are discernible. *Rich Kolasa*

Goodyear FG-1D Bureau Number 92508 was completed in May 1945. It has been in the possession of various private collectors since World War II. Currently it resides at the Military Aviation Museum, Virginia Beach, Virginia. *Rich Kolasa*

Emblazoned with checkerboard patterns on the cowling and the vertical tail, Goodyear FG-1D Bureau Number (BuNo) 67089 "Skyboss" executes a flyby. This plane has a noticeable fairing on the tail-gear doors just aft of the wheel to reduce drag. The streamlined fairings fastened to the bottoms of the pylons were normally installed when bombs or stores were not mounted on the pylons. *Rich Kolasa*

Several panels are removed from the cowling and forward fuselage of a Corsair, revealing details of the Pratt & Whitney R-2800-8 Double Wasp engine (left) and equipment in the engine-accessory compartment (right). In that compartment, the green, contoured object to the front is the left intercooler duct and carburetor air-box assembly. The yellow object is the oil tank. *Rich Kolasa*

As the Allies pushed their way back across the Pacific, the shape of the war changed. Japanese fighters, which early in the war were feared for their air-to-air prowess, were now rarely seen. Those that were encountered were less likely to engage in air-to-air combat, the type of combat for which the Corsair was designed. This was not to mean that the Corsair was rendered obsolete -- far from it -- but its role was evolving. Ground strike capabilities became increasingly important in the role of the Corsair.

Rather than the R-2800-18W of the F4U-1D, the F4U-4 was powered by the R-2800-42W, capable of generating 2,450-horsepower with water injection. The increased power brought with it increased heat, requiring the addition of an air scoop at the bottom of the cowl. To harness this power, a four-blade Hamilton Standard was used rather than the three-blade unit found on previous Corsair models. These changes raised the top speed to 448 miles per hour, and the rate of climb, according to March 1946 Navy testing, to over 3,000 feet per minute at 4,000 feet altitude, was a significant increase.

Inside, the cockpit was dramatically redesigned, for the first time having a floor, rather than merely foot troughs. At the same time, the cockpit side panels were revised and the seat itself redesigned. Part of that redesign included forming the seat back from armor plate.

Reflecting the increased importance of ground strike capabilities, the pylons beneath the center wing section were reinforced to accommodate 11.75-inch Tiny Tim rockets. Modifications also allowed the mounting of 100- to 250-pound bombs on the zero-length rocket stubs on the outer wing panels.

Produced concurrently with the F4U-4 was the F4U-4B, which was armed with four 20 mm M3 cannons. As with the earlier 20 mm-armed Corsairs, the ammunition capacity for the 20 mm rounds was considerably less than .50-caliber capacity, being 924 vs. 2,400 rounds.

The hard point arrangement of the 20 mm-armed Corsairs varied from that of F4U-4, with the stub pylons mounted in a staggered arrangement. Only 140 of the F4U-4B were produced, compared to 2,196 standard F4U-4. Even fewer were the photoreconnaissance version, the F4U-4P, which numbered only eleven. This aircraft had a camera mounted in the rear fuselage, and windows permitted photos to be taken out of the left side of the fuselage or bottom of the aircraft.

Vought assembled five prototype XF4U-4s, the precursor to the F4U-4. These planes were similar in design to the F4U-1D except for the addition of the powerful Pratt & Whitney R-2800-18W engine, a redesigned cowling with an air scoop in the chin, and a four-bladed Hamilton Standard propeller. Seen here is the second XF4U-4, BuNo 80760, at the Naval Air Test Center, Naval Air Station Patuxent River, Maryland, on January 26, 1945. *National Museum of Naval Aviation*

This photo and the following two depict an aircraft identified in the original captions as an F4U-4 on October 11, 1944. However, the presence of the number 759 on the underside of the wingtips suggests that this plane actually was the first XF4U-4, BuNo 80759. *National Archives and Records Administration*

The same plane is viewed from aft, appearing from this angle very similar to an F4U-1D. *National Archives and Records Administration*

Faintly visible from this angle is a feature that began with the XF4U-4 and was present on both sides of the plane: just aft of the cowl flaps and slightly above the level of the wing is a recess in the fuselage to accommodate two exhaust pipes, which were moved up to this position and would remain so on the production F4U-4s. On each side of the plane, a sole exhaust pipe remained in the lower position originally occupied by three exhaust pipes.
National Archives and Records Administration

A Pratt & Whitney R-2800-18W C-Series engine, the F4U-4's powerplant, is viewed from the right side in a December 1, 1944 photograph. To the right are the propeller shaft; the gear-reduction housing with the two distributors and the magneto on top of it; the two rows of cylinders; and, to the rear, engine accessories and the supercharger. *National Archives and Records Administration*

This photograph dated November 30, 1944, shows the cockpit of an F4U-4, with emphasis on the instrument panel, the Mk.8 reflector gun sight atop the instrument panel, and the control stick. There now was a new panel below the instrument panel with gun-charging controls and other items. To the front of the gun sight is a flat piece of armored glass, located behind the windshield; this flat glass also acted as a reflector for the gun sight. Significantly, there now was a floor for the cockpit.
National Archives and Records Administration

As seen in a November 30, 1944 view of the right side of an F4U-4 cockpit, the arrangement of the compartment had been drastically revised, with a new model of pilot's seat and new consoles. The right console had circuit breakers on the side, electrical controls were on the slanted forward surface, and radio controls were on the aft surface. The pilot's seat now consisted of a metal pan and a back formed from armor plate. *National Archives and Records Administration*

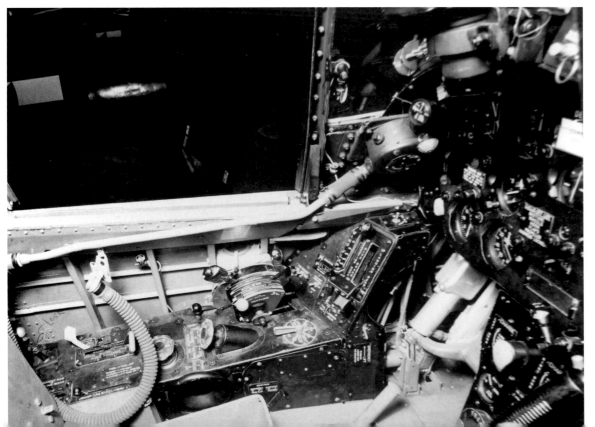

The left side of an F4U-4 cockpit is shown in another November 30, 1944 photograph. On the rear part of the surface of the console are trim controls, the fuel selector, and the wing-fold control. Above the fuel selector is the throttle quadrant. On the nearly-vertical forward face of the console are controls for the wing flaps, the landing gear, and the dive brakes. *National Archives and Records Administration*

The F4U-4B was similar to the F4U-4 except it was armed with two 20 mm cannons in each wing instead of three .50-caliber machine guns. This example, assigned to VF-42, has suffered a mishap and is about to go over the side of the carrier USS *Randolph* (CV-15) on February 22, 1947. *National Museum of Naval Aviation*

An offshoot of the F4U-4 was the F4U-4P photoreconnaissance aircraft, of which eleven examples were completed. Their primary identifying characteristic was the bulge in the left side of the fuselage aft of the cockpit to accommodate an oblique camera. That feature is visible at and around the bottom half of the star in the national insignia. A sliding door in the bulge was opened when the camera was in operation. There also were provisions for mounting a vertical reconnaissance camera in the rear of the fuselage when the mission dictated. *National Museum of Naval Aviation*

In an updated version of the F4U-2 night-fighter Corsair, F4U-4 Bureau Numbers 80764 and 97361 were converted to radar-equipped night fighters designated F4U-4N. Like the F4U-2, the F4U-4Ns had radar pods mounted on the right wings. In the case of the F4U-4N, the radar was the APS-6. This APS-6 mockup was photographed on November 16, 1944. *National Archives and Records Administration*

The APS-6 radar mockup is seen from the left side with the radome removed, exposing the parabolic antenna and dipole within. *National Archives and Records Administration*

Mockups of a radar scope and control box are shown on an F4U-4N instrument panel. The APS-6 radar scope is the dark object at the top center, and the APS-4 console-type control box is below it.
National Archives and Records Administration

The left side of an F4U-4N cockpit is depicted, showing the pilot's auxiliary radar control unit, the small black box with the large knob on top, and an electrical coupling on the rear that is mounted on the outboard side of the throttle quadrant. The photo was taken on November 16, 1944.
National Archives and Records Administration

One of the aircraft converted to an F4U-4N, BuNo 80764, is seen from the front, and it is displaying a white radome containing the APS-6 radar. The photo is dated September 18, 1947. *National Museum of Naval Aviation*

Yet another change in power plant came with the introduction of the next model of Corsair, the F4U-5. The new engine, the R-2800-32W "E"-series, was longer, featuring a two-stage variable-speed supercharger, requiring the already-long nose of the Corsair to be lengthened ten inches. The aircraft was thus 34-feet, 6.15-inches long. This length was shared with the later AU-1, but as stated is longer than the 33-feet, 8.25-inches of the F4U-4 and F4U-7.

Even more air was required for the new engine, so the cowl scoop configuration was changed, with twin cheek scoops replacing the chin scoop of the F4U-4. The cowl flap configuration was changed as well. The new engine gave the F4U-5 a top speed of 470 mph, making it the fastest Vought-built Corsair model.

While earlier models of the Corsair had fabric-covered outer wing panels, the F4U-5 was the first model to be fully sheathed in metal. The pilot's boarding step, previously located on the inboard right flap, was replaced by a retractable step in the right side of the fuselage. The canopy was raised slightly, with a small fairing being added to the fuselage spine in order to mate the latter to the new canopy.

A centerline stores pylon returned to the Corsair with the F4U-5. Although the twin pylons beneath the wing center section were retained, the new centerline pylon added a further 2,000 pounds of capacity. Integral armament was four M3 20 mm automatic cannons with 924 rounds, as had been with the F4U-4B. This meant that the arrangement of the four stub pylons on the outer wing panel of the two types were similar as well.

The XF4U-5 first flew on April 4, 1946, and the initial flight of a production F4U-5 was made on May 12, 1947. Production of the F4U-5 series totaled 568 aircraft, of which 233 were the base model, 214 were the F4U-5N night fighter variant, 101 were winterized night fighters, the F4U-5NL, and thirty were the F4U-5P reconnaissance variant.

The night fighters were equipped with AN/APS-19 or -19A radar sets on the leading edge of the right wing, as well as an autopilot and radio altimeter. Flash suppressors on the guns and flame dampeners on the engine exhaust stubs protected the pilot's night vision.

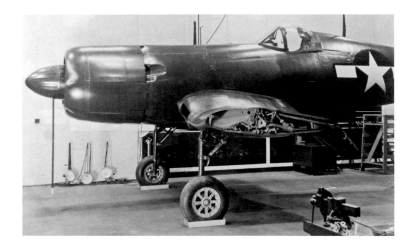

As the end of World War II drew near, the Navy decided to keep upgraded versions of the Corsair in production after the war. The new Pratt & Whitney R-2800-32W radial engine with a sidewheel supercharger was to be the powerplant of the first of these postwar Corsairs. Toward this end, three F4U-4s were converted to XF4U-5 prototypes. This March 3, 1945 photo of an XF4U-5 shows it with a mockup partial propeller with a spinner that did not make it into production. Note the higher position of the upper exhausts compared with the F4U-4. *National Archives and Records Administration*

As seen in a frontal view, the cowling of the XF4U-5 was not round, like those of its predecessors, but was wider at the bottom to accommodate two air inlets for the twin auxiliary blowers. These "cheek" inlets replaced the chin inlet of the F4U-4. *National Archives and Records Administration*

The XF4U-5 is seen from the left front. Although difficult to discern in these photos of the plane, the cowl flaps had been redesigned, with flaps present on the bottom and the upper quadrants of the fuselage but with a gap in the flaps below the upper exhausts and at the top of the fuselage. *National Archives and Records Administration*

A mockup of the Pratt & Whitney R-2800-32W for an XF4U-5 Corsair is observed from the right side in this February 8, 1945 photograph. The exhausts are fabricated from wood in an effort to establish their proper shapes with reference to the changed layout of the engine, supercharger, and cowling. The light-colored object between the supercharger and the firewall appears to be a mockup of part of the air duct for the auxiliary blowers. *National Archives and Records Administration*

Vought completed a total of 223 F4U-5s and its night-fighting and reconnaissance variants. F4U-5 BuNo 121794 is seen in a January 8, 1948 photo. This was the first F4U-5 to be tested at NATC Patuxent River, Maryland. This model of Corsair was armed with four 20 mm cannons and had a longer fuselage than the F4U-4. *Navy History and Heritage Command*

This is an early-production Vought F4U-5 Corsair, BuNo 121796, at NATC Patuxent River, Maryland, August 8, 1948, with wings folded. Note the Naval Air Test Center markings on the wing. Starting with the F4U-5, the outer wing panels had all-metal skin, dispensing with the partially fabric covering of Corsairs up to the F4U-4. This change to metal resulted in increased speed because of the reduction in drag, metal being smoother than fabric. *Navy History and Heritage Command*

In this photo of an F4U-5, the interruption in the cowl flaps below the upper exhaust pipes is evident. Visible through the sliding canopy is the pilot's shoulder harness and its mounting bar below the headrest. *National Museum of Naval Aviation*

This F4U-5, BuNo 121796, was the fourth plane in that series, the first being BuNo 121793. Visible below the trailing edge of the right wing is a feature that was new with that model of Corsair: a retractable step. When not in use, it was pushed up into the fuselage, and the bottom of the step fit flush with the fuselage skin. *National Museum of Naval Aviation*

F4U-5 BuNo 122032 is parked on a hardstand at NATC, Patuxent River, Maryland, on November 18, 1949. NATC markings are on the vertical tail; the fuselage code of the last three letters of the BuNo, 032, is on the fuselage; and "FT" is marked to the front of the windscreen. The national insignia is the type with the red stripes on the white side bars, introduced in 1947. *National Museum of Naval Aviation*

More than half of the F4U-5s were completed as night-fighters: the F4U-5N and the F4U-5NL, a winterized version. Both versions carried an AN/APS-19 or -19A radar in a fairing and radome on the right wing. Flash suppressors were fitted on the muzzles of the four M3 20 mm cannons. As seen in this June 19, 1949 photograph of a very early F4U-5N, BuNo 121853, a curved flame shield now was fitted to the fuselage aft of the upper exhausts to protect the pilot's eyes from the glare of the exhausts at night. The plane bears the NATC markings of the Naval Air Test Station. *Navy History and Heritage Command*

F4U-5N BuNo 124493 is viewed from below while serving as a test plane. The paint scheme was Sea Blue with Yellow on select areas on the undersides. This was one of the Corsairs transferred to Honduran Air Force in 1956. From 1987 to 1996, this plane was displayed at the Royal New Zealand Air Force Museum in Christchurch. In 1996, a private collector in Australia acquired it for restoration to airworthiness. *National Museum of Naval Aviation*

An F4U-5N assigned to VMF(N)-513 is parked at an unidentified airfield in 1952. A drop tank is mounted on the left pylon. Tires with different tread patterns are mounted on the main landing gear. *National Museum of Naval Aviation*

A beautifully restored F4U-5N cuts through the air during a flight in the not-distant past. This Corsair, BuNo 124692, is part of the collection of the Collings Foundation in Stow, Massachusetts. Note the two radio altimeter antennas, shaped like inverted Ts, under the fuselage, and the VHF mast antenna mounted on top of the tail cone of the fuselage. *Rich Kolasa*

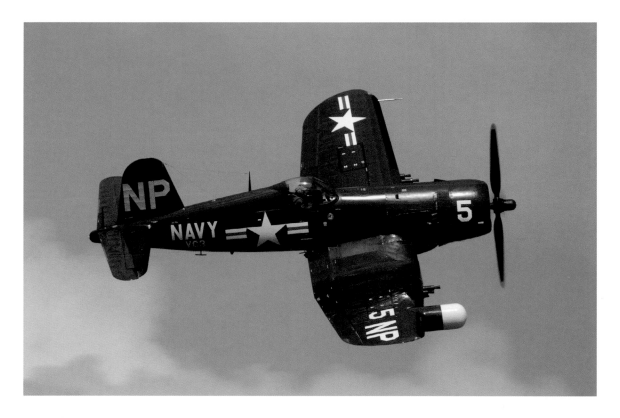

The Collings Foundation's F4U-5N is viewed from the right side as its engine is being run up. The canopy on the F4U-5N as well as the F4U-5 and F4U-5P was taller than that on the F4U-4. Note the retractable step toward the bottom of the fuselage aft of the trailing edge of the wing. *Rich Kolasa*

The Collings Foundation's F4U-5N, BuNo 124692, is parked on a hardstand. The flame shield above and aft of the upper exhausts is clearly visible. Although this plane was built as an F4U-5N, it carries nomenclature stencils under the horizontal stabilizers for the F4U-5NL, the winterized version of the F4U-5N. To replicate a -5NL plane, real or imitation deicer boots were applied to the leading edges of the wings, elevators, and vertical fin. *Rich Kolasa*

This frontal view of the Collings Foundation's F4U-5N provides a close-up view of the Hamilton Standard 6541 Hydromatic A-0 propeller, with oval Hamilton Standard logo decals and yellow stencils and tips on the blades. Note the small fins on the insides of the cheek air inlets. During the postwar years this Corsair served with the Honduran Air Force. *Rich Kolasa*

A final photo of the Collings Foundation's F4U-5N emphasizes the impressive mass of the lowered wing flaps. Details also are available for the flash suppressors on the 20 mm cannons, the propellers, the cowling and flame shield, and the main landing gear. *Rich Kolasa*

CHAPTER 9
AU-1

Originally designated the XF4U-6, the AU-1 was the F4U-5 optimized for the ground attack role. The XF4U-6 first flew on January 31, 1952. Twenty-five pieces of armor were added to protect the pilot, engine, and fuel tanks. The oil coolers were repositioned, affording greater protection.

Because high-altitude capability was not required of a ground attack aircraft, the aircraft was powered by a R-2800-83W engine with single-stage, manually controlled supercharger. This engine did not require the volume of air needed by the R-2800-32W of the F4U-5, so the check scoops were deleted, although their telltale bulges in the cowl ring remained.

As with the F4U-5, the primary armament of the AU-1 were four 20 mm automatic cannons, mounted two per wing. However, the gun control circuitry was changed, allowing the guns to be fired either all four in unison, or in pairs, one each from both wings. The latter configuration cut the firepower per pass in half, but doubled the firing time.

Each outer wing panel of the AU-1 was fitted with five pylons, allowing bombs up to 250 pounds or five-inch rockets to be carried on each station. By utilizing only the inner, outer, and middle pylon on each wing, the bomb load could include 500-pound bombs on each of these three positions. The centerline pylon and twin pylons beneath the wing center section introduced on the F4U-5 were retained as well.

Only 111 AU-1s were built, all between February 7, and October 10, 1952. The aircraft were initially supplied to the Marine Corps, and the Marines transferred twenty-five of their aircraft to the French for use in Indochina. The Marines would also transfer additional AU-1s to the Navy, which used the aircraft to equip Navy Reserve squadrons.

The Vought AU-1 was a ground-attack version of the Corsair, based on the F4U-5 airframe. The prototype plane for this model, shown here, was a plane originally designated XF4U-6 but redesignated XAU-1 before it was delivered. It was converted from F4U-5N BuNo 124665. A key feature for identifying these ground-attack Corsairs was the set of five pylons under each outer-wing section. Each pylon could hold a bomb weighing up to 500 pounds or a five-inch high-velocity aerial rocket. *National Archives and Records Administration*

A total of 111 production AU-1s, including this example, were delivered between February and October 1952. Although in most respects similar in exterior appearance to the F4U-5, the AU-1's upper exhausts occupied the same area on the fuselage as the F4U-5's, just above the leading edge of the wings. On the turtledeck are a blade antenna and a mast antenna for the AN/ARC-27 radio. *National Archives and Records Administration*

Vought AU-1s are undergoing final assembly. These Corsairs retained the same cowling shapes as the F4U-5, wider at the bottom when viewed from the front, but lacked the two cheek intakes on the interior of the cowling. This is because the AU-1 was equipped with the Pratt & Whitney R-2800-83W engine, which had a single-stage supercharger and did not require the two cheek intakes. The planes in the background have "MARINES" marked on the bottoms of the left wings. *National Archives and Records Administration*

Nearly complete AU-1s are nearing the end of the Vought production line. The lack of cheek intakes inside the cowlings is evident. The second plane in line is marked "NAVY" on the underside of the left wing. *National Archives and Records Administration*

Vought AU-1 BuNo 133843 with USMC markings is parked on a tarmac. The Marines flew AU-1s in Korea during the latter part of the war in that country. Noticeable through the windscreen is a prominent gun sight. *National Museum of Naval Aviation*

A Marine Corps AU-1, BuNo 129320, cruises high above a populated area. A noticeable antiglare panel is present on the upper part of the forward fuselage and cowling, the bottom of which is a straight line with a downward angle toward the front. *National Museum of Naval Aviation*

The last production model of the Corsair to roll off the Vought assembly line was the F4U-7. Although developed and produced expressly for the French Navy, the aircraft nevertheless were assigned US Navy Bureau Numbers 133652 through 133731 and 133819 through 133832. This was a result of the US government's Foreign Military Sales policies.

To the observer, the F4U-7 appeared to be an F4U-4 with AU-1 wings installed. The aircraft was powered by the R-2800-43W engine, similar to that used in the late F4U-4, and thus requiring the chin scoop at the base of the cowl ring. The high canopy of the F4U-5 was used, as well as the spine-top fairing to blend the canopy to the fuselage.

The under-wing weapons stores of the F4U-7 were the same as those of the AU-1, with five pylons under each outer wing section, a centerline pylon, and a pair of pylons beneath the wing center section. After delivery, some of the F4U-7s were equipped to fire wire-guided SS-11 air-to-surface missiles.

The first flight of the F4U-7 was made on July 2, 1952, above Dallas, where it had been built. Vought operations had relocated from Connecticut to the Lone Star State during production of the F4U-5 model, and all subsequent Corsairs came from the Dallas assembly lines. The Navy Bureau of Aeronautics had requested this relocation, an effort to move the plant, a prime contractor for Navy aircraft, to a less vulnerable inland area, with a more efficient plant layout and greater space for testing forthcoming jet-powered aircraft. The government-owned, contractor-operated plant in Dallas, utilized by North American Aviation during World War II, was chosen to be Vought's new home, with the move made in 1948–49.

The French flew the F4U-7 from land bases as well as their carriers *Lafayette, Arromanches*, and *Bois Belleau*. F4U-7s were involved in combat in Indochina, the Suez, and Algeria.

The final model of Corsair to leave the assembly lines was the F4U-7, all ninety-four of which were produced for the *Marine Nationale* (French Navy). These Corsairs served with the French from the early 1950s until the final ones were retired in 1964. The F4U-7 had the tall canopy like the F4U-5; five pylons under each outer-wing section, like the AU-1; and had the same overall length as the F4U-4: 33 feet, 8.25 inches. The engine was the Pratt & Whitney R-2800-43W. The insignia of the French Navy is on the bottom of the right wing. *National Museum of Naval Aviation*

In French Naval service, the F4U-7s were marked with US Navy Bureau Numbers. On this plane photographed during 1952, nomenclature marking "F4U-7" and the the BuNo 133693 are marked in white to the front of the horizontal stabilizer. A retractable step and an inverted T-shaped radio-altimeter antenna are present. *National Museum of Naval Aviation*

An F4U-7, BuNo 133699, is viewed from above during a flight in 1952. The pattern of the exhaust smudging on the side of the fuselage is noticeable. Of particular interest is the fairing attached to the top of the turtledeck to the rear: a feature introduced starting with the F4U-5 to compensate for the higher sliding canopy of that model. *National Museum of Naval Aviation*

CHAPTER 11
The Ultimate Corsair, the F2G

While the F4U-7 was in fact the final version of the Corsair built, leaving the factory in 1952, it could be argued that it was not the pinnacle of Corsair development. That title would likely go not to any Vought-built Corsair, but rather a World War II-era model produced by Goodyear, the F2G-1.

The F2G was a marriage of the Corsair airframe with the powerful R-4360 engine, the most powerful production American aircraft engine of World War II. These efforts began to come to fruition in March 1943, when F4U-1 Bureau Number 02460 was provided to Pratt & Whitney for proof of concept. Fitted with the then-experimental XR-4360, the huge 28-cylinder, 3,000-horsepower gave the Corsair an impressive rate of climb.

Encouraged by these tests, the Navy tasked Goodyear with developing two production variants of the R-4360-powered aircraft. The F2G-1 was to be a land-based aircraft, while the F2G-2 would have hydraulically folding wings, a tail hook, and slightly smaller propeller, all to permit carrier operations.

Perhaps even more noticeable than the extended nose and air scoop of the F2G was the bubble canopy, adapted from the P-47D. This made the F2G the only Corsair variant with a true bubble top, with the associated improved vision. To offset the torque of the big engine and the loss of the fuselage spine, the vertical tail of the F2G was taller than that of other Corsairs.

While the rated maximum speed of the F2G was only modestly increased over that of the F4U-4, the F2G's 4,400-feet-per-minute rate of climb was a thirty-three-percent increase over that of the 3,340-feet-per-minute of the F4U-4.

In March 1944, orders were placed for 408 of the F2G-1 and ten of the F2G-2. However, Goodyear taking over the cancelled Brewster production of Corsairs prevented Goodyear production of F4U-4 equivalents, and also delayed the introduction of the F2G. As a result, only five of each F2G-1 and F2G-2 were completed when the contract was cancelled at the end of World War II. Though delivered to the Navy, by 1947, the F2G aircraft were being disposed of as surplus, or expended as training aids. In part, this was because during the delay in beginning production, the Grumman F8F Bearcat had been introduced, providing an aircraft with many of the attributes found desirable in the F2G.

The Goodyear F2G model was to have been a high-performance, high-altitude interceptor capable of defeating Japanese kamikaze aircraft. It was intended that there would be two types: the F2G-1 land-based interceptor, with manually folding wings; and a carrier-based F2G-2, with hydraulically folding wings, smaller-diameter propeller, and an arresting hook. Power was to be provided by the Pratt & Whitney XR-4360 radial engine rated at 3,000 horsepower. Seven prototypes of the land-based version, designated XF2G-1, were produced. This photo, taken at NAS Patuxent River on February 2, 1945, depicts one of them, BuNo 14691, which was equipped with a bubble canopy and bore a large number 9 on the cowling. *National Museum of Naval Aviation*

Because of the decline of the threat of kamikaze attacks as 1945 progressed, the order for F2Gs was slashed and only five production F2G-1 interceptors were completed. This example, BuNo 88454, was the first of those planes. It bears the markings of the National Air Test Center at NAS Patuxent River. The F2Gs featured a prominent air scoop to the upper rear of the cowling. Because of the extreme torque of the engine and propeller during takeoffs and landings, a tall vertical fin was used, along with an auxiliary rudder below the stock rudder, which automatically turned 12.5 degrees to the right when the landing gear was lowered, to compensate for the torque. F2G-1 88454 has been preserved in various collections over the years, and most recently was at the Museum of Flying in Seattle, Washington. *National Museum of Naval Aviation*

CHAPTER 12
The Corsair Sees Combat

One of the earliest F4U-1s makes a flight out of Norfolk in July 1942. The Brownscope rear-view periscope that was a standard item on early-production F4U-1s is faintly visible above the top of the windscreen. Later in F4U-1 production, the periscope was discontinued, and a rear-view mirror was mounted under a blister on the top front panel of the sliding canopy. *National Museum of Naval Aviation*

Carrier qualification trials of the Corsair began on September 25, 1942, aboard the USS *Sangamon*. Carrier landings of the Corsair was at times problematic, as were many aircraft, especially early on. Adjustments of the landing gear and revision of the tail hook resolved most of these issues, however the Navy Commander of Aircraft Pacific decreed that "In order to simplify spares problem and insure flexibility in carrier operations, present practice in Pacific is to assign all Corsairs to Marines and equip FightRons on medium and light carriers with Hellcats."

While spare part logistics were the problem for US carriers, British carriers had another problem—the Corsair was simply too big. With folded wings the Corsair was 16-feet, 3-inches tall; specified clearance on the British carriers was 15-feet, 10-inches. In order to remedy this conflict, first Brewster designed shorter wood wing tips, and later Andover Kent Aviation engineered fiberglass replacements, which began to be installed on Commonwealth Corsairs in February 1944. Two months later it was learned that due to changes in specifications of both British

aircraft carriers and the Corsair, the aircraft was still too tall, and Brewster designed an even shorter fiberglass wingtip, which were retrofitted to Corsair II and Corsair III aircraft, and were factory-installed on the Corsair IV.

Owing to the decision of the Navy to assign the Corsair to land-based units, almost a quarter of the Goodyear FG-1 production had their wings locked in the open position. When in December 1944 the Corsair was again assigned to US Navy carriers, the wing folding feature returned.

During World War II, the US Navy flew 64,051 operational sorties with the Corsair, although only 9,581 were from carriers. With 2,140 claimed kills against 189 losses, the Corsair earned an impressive 11:1 kill ratio. Additionally, 15,621 tons of ordnance were delivered by Corsairs during the conflict.

While after World War II some Corsairs were declared surplus, most were used to reequip Hellcat squadrons with Corsairs, and still others were placed in "mothball" storage.

Marine Fighter Squadron 124 (VMF-124) was part of the Cactus Air Force, a collection of USN, USMC, and New Zealand land-based squadrons involved in the defense of Guadalcanal. Here, the first F4U-1 Corsair to land at Guadalcanal is warming its engine on February 13, 1943. Note the bulge on the top of the late-style canopy. *National Museum of Naval Aviation*

An F4U-1 assigned to VF-17 "Jolly Rogers" is on the elevator of the escort carrier USS *Charger* (CVE-30) on March 8, 1943. A practice-bomb dispenser is mounted on the pylon on the folded left wing. The machine-gun apertures are taped over, and the landing light is visible toward the wingtip. *National Museum of Naval Aviation*

Vought F4U-1 17-F-6 of VF-17 catches a wire upon landing on USS *Charger* (CVE-30) during training exercises in February 1943. The Corsair was painted in the Blue Gray over Light Gray camouflage scheme. This photo illustrates the tendency of the F4U-1 to bounce hard upon landing, due to an overly stiff main landing gear. Eventually, this problem would be solved. *National Museum of Naval Aviation*

During early 1943, personnel relax along a flightline of F4U-1s of VMF-124 "Rainbow Squadron" on Guadalcanal. Shortly after, this squadron would be redubbed the "Bulldog Squadron." These Corsairs have small, black aircraft numbers on the fronts of the cowlings. In the background is a fuel truck. *National Museum of Naval Aviation*

Vought F4U-1 17-F-12 of VF-17 has come to an arrested stop on the flight deck of USS *Bunker Hill* (CV-17) on July 11, 1943. This plane has received the updated national insignia authorized from June to September 1943, featuring white side bars and a red border. On the cowling is the pirate flag insignia of the "Jolly Rogers" squadron. *Navy History and Heritage Command*

An F4U-1, fuselage code 17-F-10, of VF-17, has just crashed on the flight deck of an aircraft carrier around 1943. Early on in its operational career, the F4U-1s experienced problems while undergoing carrier-qualification trials, occasioned by various performance deficiencies, including premature stalling of the left wing, poor pilot visibility, and inflexibility in the main landing gear. It was the engineering and maintenance staff of VF-17 that finally solved the problem of stiff landing gear by discovering the optimum balance of oil and pressurized air in the oleo struts. *National Museum of Naval Aviation*

The main landing gear of F4U-1 17-F-18 apparently has become snagged on an arrestor wire, and the plane is perilously close to flipping over on USS *Bunker Hill* on July 21, 1943. Running laterally at intervals on the flight deck are the steel tie-down strips, with U-shaped perforations for attaching stays to aircraft to secure them in place while parked on deck.
National Archives and Records Administration

Another F4U-1 assigned to VF-17, code 17-F-24, has overturned on the flight deck of the carrier USS *Bunker Hill* (CV-17), causing damage to the propeller and, no doubt, to the vertical tail and other structures. A rare view is available of the rear landing-gear doors. There were several successive models of doors for the various Corsairs, and these are the early type, with lateral ribs on the interior. These doors also have cutouts to allow clearance for the tail wheel when mounted on longer landing gear. *National Museum of Naval Aviation*

At an airstrip at Munda on New Georgia in the Solomon Islands on August 26, 1943, an F4U-1 churns up dust as it taxis on a sandy runway. Aside from the national insignia with borderless white side bars, the only markings visible on the plane are the number 91 painted on both of the forward main landing-gear doors. *National Museum of Naval Aviation*

The pilot of F4U-1 BuNo 17493 of VMF-214 prepares to hand his parachute pack up to the ground crewman on the wing, at Turtle Bay Airfield on Espiritu Santo, September 11, 1943. Marine Fighter Squadron 214 was the renowned "Black Sheep Squadron," commanded by Maj. Gregory "Pappy" Boyington. Note the red border around the national insignia, the bulged top front panel of the sliding canopy, and the ample mud spattered on the underside of the Corsair. *National Museum of Naval Aviation*

A British pilot is seated in a Corsair I, the British version of the Vought F4U-1, while training to qualify in that aircraft at Naval Air Station Quonset Point, Rhode Island, in September 1943. On the fuselage is the insignia of the Naval Air Training Center (NATC), Pensacola, Florida, featuring a cartoon duck mascot, "J. Gosling." Note the recessed step with a sprung cover above the wing. *Navy History and Heritage Command*

Vought F4U-1s are having their engines warmed up at an airfield on Vella Lavella in the Solomon Islands on November 1, 1943. At least the nearest three planes have the late-style sliding canopies with the bulge on the forward top clear panel, to provide space for a rear-view mirror. No markings are visible except for two-digit numbers on the forward main landing-gear doors; and, on the third plane from the left, the top of a white two-digit number is visible above the wing. *National Museum of Naval Aviation*

Pratt & Whitney R-2800 engines for Vought Corsairs are undergoing disassembly, cleaning, and preservation at an engine-overhaul shop on Guadalcanal on December 13, 1943. The shed in the right background has a sign identifying it as the cleaning shop. Also to the right, several mechanics are working on an R-2800 engine assembly complete with its nose cowl assembly, cowl flaps, and engine mount. *National Archives and Records Administration*

Naval personnel survey the wreckage of F4U-1A BuNo 56262, which had the dubious honor of being the first plane to crashland on Green Island, Papua New Guinea, following its occupation by Allied forces in February 1944. The outboard end of the left wing was demolished. The last three digits of the Bureau Number are marked in white on the fuselage next to the national insignia. *National Archives and Records Administration*

Three F4U-1As (the tail of one is visible under the left wing of number 255) of the Fourth Marine Air Wing are bound for a strike against Japanese forces in the Marshall Islands in June 1944. These planes are armed with 1,000-pound bombs on Brewster bomb racks, and they have the early-style F4U-1A canopies with the two upper fore-and-aft frames. *National Archives and Records Administration*

A Vought F4U-2 night-fighter takes off from the escort carrier USS *Windham Bay* (CVE-92) bound for a mission over Saipan on July 12, 1944. This plane was assigned to VMF(N)-532. The fairing for the AIA radar antenna is visible on the right wing, and the canopy is of the early type, with two fore-and-aft frame members toward the top. *National Museum of Naval Aviation*

Corsairs of VMF-114 were prominent in the battle for Peleliu, in the Palau Islands, in September 1944. These planes were heavily engaged in air-support missions against Bloody Nose Ridge. This Goodyear FG-1 with a Duramold drop tank full of napalm is preparing to take off for the very short hop to its target. Light-colored tape covers the machine-gun apertures on the leading edge of the wing, to reduce drag and keep out dust and foreign objects. *National Museum of Naval Aviation*

A damage-control party douses flames from a drop tank that fell off the Corsair Mk.II to the right and exploded on the flight deck of a British aircraft carrier on September 18, 1944. Earlier, the plane had taken off on a raid against railroad installations at Sigli, Sumatra, but had to make an emergency landing, the force of which shook the drop tank loose. This ship was one of the two Royal Navy carriers involved in that raid, *Indomitable* and *Victorious*. *National Archives and Records Administration*

Mechanics of the Fourth Marine Air Wing are servicing a line of Corsairs at an airfield on Engebi Island, Eniwetok Atoll, on September 6, 1944. To the front of the planes, lights are rigged on poles to allow around-the-clock maintenance of the planes. All four Corsairs are F4U-1As with the early-type canopy. *National Archives and Records Administration*

The right wing of an F4U-1D has been secured in a vertical position for servicing the machine guns and ammunition. One end of a jury strut fastened to the wing to immobilize it in this position is visible below the aviation ordnanceman's right elbow. He is installing a box full of .50-caliber ammunition into the wing. The top of the box will form part of the wing surface. The boxes are numbered; the one the AO is handling is number 4. Toward the bottom of the photo are the receivers of the three right machine guns and their feed chutes. *National Archives and Records Administration*

A Vought F4U-1D assigned to VF-5 is warming its engine on the flight deck of USS *Franklin* (CV-13) in March 1945. On the vertical tail is a white diamond symbol. This was the "G" symbol ("G" standing for Group) for the *Franklin*'s air group. There also was a white diamond symbol on the outer part of the right wing, not visible from this angle. *National Museum of Naval Aviation*

Airedales are spotting an F4U-1D of VBF-6 on the flight deck of the *Essex*-class carrier USS *Hancock* (CV-19) on March 21, 1945. This was at a time when the *Hancock*'s air group had been striking targets in the Japanese home islands. The day before this photo was taken, *Hancock* had been the target of a kamikaze attack, suffering damage to her flight deck. *Hancock*'s "G" symbol was a diagonal white stripe, with the high end to the front. *National Museum of Naval Aviation*

This F4U-1D assigned to VMF-512 was the victim of a mishap while it was being loaded aboard the escort carrier USS *Gilbert Islands* (CVE-107) at Naval Air Station San Diego on March 11, 1945, crashing upside down on a dock. In addition to the EE64 code on the fuselage, a small number 5 and a larger number 27 are on the cowling. On the forward doors of the main landing gear is stenciled the number 64, with a number 5 chalked on the doors as well. *National Museum of Naval Aviation*

In mid-April 1945, USMC F4U-1D Corsairs that have flown to Iwo Jima from the Marianas Islands pause temporarily for refueling before embarking on the final leg of their flight, to Okinawa. Some of the Corsairs have large, stylized numbers on the cowlings. In the middle background is a Consolidated PB4Y-2 Privateer; in the left background is a B-29 Superfortress, while Mount Suribachi looms in the distance. *National Museum of Naval Aviation*

Aviation ordnancemen are making final adjustments to high-velocity aerial rockets on the right wing of an F4U-1D on an *Essex*-class aircraft carrier prior to a raid on Okinawa in or before April 1945. The arrow on the vertical tail was the "G" symbol of the air group of USS *Bunker Hill* (CV-17). The aircraft number 168 is on the cowling and the vertical fin, and the one-inch-high Bureau Number on the vertical fin appears to be 57757. *National Museum of Naval Aviation*

An F4U-1C Corsair armed with four 20 mm cannons is parked at a base on Okinawa in spring 1945. Panels have been removed from the fuselage aft of the cowling and the wing root, revealing to view the disconnected air duct for the left intercooler. *National Archives and Records Administration*

An aviation ordnanceman checks the .50-caliber guns in the wing of an F6F Hellcat while an F4U-1D numbered 4 and another Corsair are spotted in the background aboard USS *Yorktown* (CV-10) on May 9, 1945. The Corsairs bear the diamond-shaped "G" symbols of the USS *Franklin*'s (CV-13) air group, the *Franklin* having left the war zone for repairs after suffering catastrophic damage in a bombing attack on March 19. Several Corsairs were able to escape from the burning carrier, finding new homes on other carriers, including these ones from VF-5. *National Museum of Naval Aviation*

Airdales prepare to haul away an F4U-1D that flipped over upon landing on the escort carrier USS *Windham Bay* (CVE-92) on May 12, 1945. The shock of the crash tore away the left front main landing-gear door, and the fairings are missing from both pylons on the center wing section, exposing to view the bomb racks. *National Museum of Naval Aviation*

The subject of this photo of personnel gathered around and atop an F4U-1C may have been a training session. The photo was taken on Okinawa on July 6, 1945. Note the two 20 mm cannon barrels at the bottom center of the photograph. *National Archives and Records Administration*

During July and August 1945, Corsairs of Bombing Fighting Squadron 6 (VBF-6), assigned to the carrier USS *Hancock* (CV-19), flew airstrikes against the Japanese home islands. In this photo taken in August of that year, two F4U-4s of VBF-6 fly in formation during a mission. They are marked with the "U" tail code of USS *Hancock*'s air group. *National Museum of Naval Aviation*

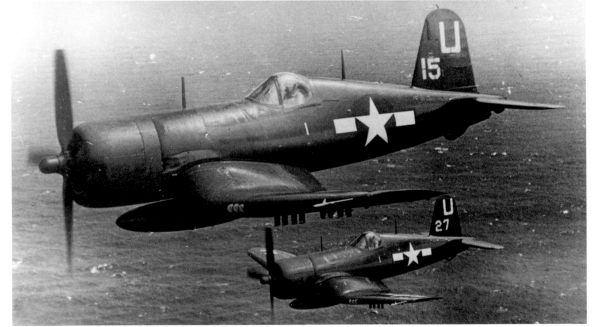

The pilot of this F4U-1D of VBF-83 has initiated the wing-fold mechanism as the plane taxis forward aboard USS *Essex* (CV-9) sometime in 1945. Of interest is the painting technique on the CV-9 "G" symbol on the vertical tail: the White paint was oversprayed onto the Sea Blue base color, with dark strips around the markings where the masking was applied and faint white overspray beyond that.
National Museum of Naval Aviation

The pilot of an F4U-1D appears to have thus far survived crashing into another Corsair aboard USS *Essex* (CV-9) in 1945. The crash has collapsed the left landing gear and the engine and cowling, severed or nearly severed the fuselage aft of the cockpit, and mangled the right wing. This plane would have been declared unsalvageable. *National Museum of Naval Aviation*

CHAPTER 13
Return to Combat

The pilot of F4U-4 fuselage code 82-BF-17, of VBF-82, is securing his plane for takeoff on USS *Randolph* (CV-15) in the Southern Drill Grounds off the Virginia Capes in June 1946. In the aftermath of World War II, the US Navy had discontinued operations of its Grumman F6F Hellcats, choosing to keep its Corsairs in service. *National Museum of Naval Aviation*

With the outbreak of war in Korea, the Corsair returned to combat. With the introduction of the MiG-15 early in the war, the Corsair, which had previously faced the piston-engined Yakovlev Yak-9, confronted an adversary best-suited for other allied fighters. The Corsair returned to a role with which it had done well in the prior conflict—that of ground attack aircraft. F4U-4s, which just entered production as World War II closed, were joined by the newer -5 Corsair as well as the specialized ground attack AU-1. Not surprisingly, the aircraft performed well in the conflict.

The US was not the only nation to use the Corsair in combat post-World War II. The French navy flew Corsairs during the First Indochina War, the first unit in the country, Flotille 14F arriving at Da Nang April 17, 1954. The Corsair was in combat over Vietnam for two months, firing more than 300 rockets, 70,000 20 mm rounds, and dropping 1.5 million pounds of bombs, much of this in support of the besieged troops at Dien Bien Phu.

French Corsairs again saw combat during the Suez Crisis as well the Algerian War, both in 1956.

In 1961, when the recently independent Tunisia attempted to force France to abandon its base at Bizerte, French Corsairs supported paratroopers in securing the base. Although the base was secured, in 1963 after the Algerian war the French base at Bizerte, Tunisia was transferred to the Tunisian government.

Final combat operations of the Corsair came during the so-called "Football War" of 1969, between Honduras and El Salvador, with pilots of both nations flying the Corsair. That conflict saw both the final kill by, as well as the last downing of, a Corsair in combat. Honduran pilot Capt. Fernando Soto downed two FG-1s, among other aircraft, on July 17, 1969.

F4U-4B BuNo 97412 is parked at Floyd Bennett Field in Brooklyn, New York, on June 27, 1947. On the cowling is the "Green Pawn" insignia of VF-4B. (This squadron was redesignated VF-42 the following year). A good view is available of the design and placement of the rocket pylons on the outer wing; these are fitted with rails for mounting subcaliber aircraft rockets (SCAR), used for practice gunnery. *National Museum of Naval Aviation*

Vought F4U-4s serving with VF-5B prepare for takeoff from USS *Coral Sea* (CVB-43) during the carrier's shakedown cruise to Guantanamo Bay, Cuba, in January 1948. Skull-and-crossbone markings and aircraft numbers are stenciled on the cowlings. *National Museum of Naval Aviation*

F4U-5 BuNo 121928, assigned at the time to VF-44, is parked with its engine running on a hardstand at Naval Air Station Norfolk, Virginia, in the spring of 1950. Note the heavy streaking from exhaust along the length of the fuselage. The tail code, F, is repeated on the bottom of the right wing. The arrestor hook is painted in black-and-white bands. *National Museum of Naval Aviation*

A Vought F4U-4B assigned to VF-54 advances on the flight deck of USS *Valley Forge* (CV-45) while other F4U-4Bs await their turn during operations off Korea on December 29, 1950. These planes are armed with rockets and have one drop tank on the right pylon. The *Valley Forge*'s fighter and attack squadrons bore the tail code "S" during the carrier's May–December 1950 deployment.

Ground crewmen are servicing an F4U-4B assigned to VMF-312 around 1950. The scene was at Nellis Air Force Base. Almost hidden in the shadow under the horizontal stablizer is the plane's Bureau Number, 62965. While serving with Marine Air Group 12, this plane was lost in Korea on August 4, 1952, when it ran out of fuel; the pilot bailed out and survived. *National Museum of Naval Aviation*

A small letter E, presumably representing a battle efficiency award, is below the windscreen of this F4U-5, BuNo 121795, photographed at Yonpo Airfield, Korea, in December 1950. At that time, this Corsair was serving with VMF-212. Bomb symbols marking thirty-three missions are to the front of the windscreen. Note the retractable step aft of the wing and the recessed step, in the open position, on the side of the cockpit. *National Museum of Naval Aviation*

Ordnance crewmen are making a final check of the weapons on an F4U-4B aboard USS *Sicily* (CVE-18) as the Corsair prepares to take off on a strike against Communist forces in Korea sometime in 1950. The plane is loaded with eight HVARs, a 500-pound bomb on the left pylon, and a drop tank or napalm bomb on the right pylon. *National Museum of Naval Aviation*

A badly damaged F4U-4P photo-recon Corsair formerly assigned to Composite Squadron 61 (VC-61), Detachment (Det) 3, on the carrier USS *Philippine Sea* (CV-47) sits in a salvage yard around 1950. The tail code of VC-61, "PP," is present. Note the open oblique-camera door at the lower part of the star on the national insignia on the fuselage.
National Museum of Naval Aviation

F4U-4B BuNo 97428, assigned to VF-114, is preparing to take off from USS *Philippine Sea* (CV-47) off Korea in February 1951. The aircraft is rigged to a catapult, the bridle of which is not visible, but the holdback rigging attached to the rear landing gear, which restrains the aircraft until the signal to launch it, is in view. The name of the pilot, Bill Williams, is stenciled over the symbols for thirty-eight bombing missions. *National Museum of Naval Aviation*

A heavily weathered F4U-4 assigned to Naval Air Reserve Training Unit (NARTU) Los Alamitos, California, flies over farmlands around 1950. The dome of the propeller hub and the tip of the vertical tail are painted white, and a partial band of yellow is on the aft part of the fuselage. The Bureau Number, 96832, is faintly visible under the horizontal stabilizer.
National Museum of Naval Aviation

A Vought F4U-4P photo-reconnaissance Corsair of VC-61, Det-H, has caught an arrestor wire on USS *Valley Forge* (CV-45) upon returning from a mission over Korea in early 1951. This plane was shot down during a mission over Wonsan Harbor on February 20, of that year, but the pilot, Lt. McDermott, was rescued by a US Navy destroyer. *National Museum of Naval Aviation*

Marine ground crewmen are attempting to rock the wings of F4U-4B BuNo 97454 in order to free its wheels, stuck in soft sand at the Seoul City Air Base in Korea on April 29, 1951. Compounding matters is the heavy load of HVARs, bombs, and centerline tank or napalm bomb. This plane was lost, with the death of its pilot, while providing covering fire for downed pilots on October 16, 1951. In the foreground is F4U-4B 63025. *National Museum of Naval Aviation*

This F4U-4B of VMF-323 flipped over during a landing on the escort carrier USS *Badoeng Strait* (CVE-116) around 1951. The crash bent the propeller, dented the underside of the cowling and the drop tanks, sheared off one of the rocket pylons on the right wing, and no doubt caused other damage to the aircraft. *National Museum of Naval Aviation*

The engine of an F4U-4B is being warmed up and the wheels restrained by wooden chocks at Airfield K-1 in Korea in 1951. This plane was assigned to Headquarters Squadron (Hedron) 12. Evidence of the blue paint that covers the aircraft is visible on the oleo struts and wheels of the main landing gear. *National Museum of Naval Aviation*

As seen from a quad 40 mm gun mount on the carrier USS *Philippine Sea* (CV-47) in 1951, F4U-4s of VF-24 are lined up on the flight deck. Also in the view are several Douglas Skyraiders, with green propeller hubs. The Corsairs have bombs mounted on the outer-wing pylons and drop tanks or napalm canisters on their center-wing pylons. *National Museum of Naval Aviation*

Munitions are stored on the edge of the flight deck next to several Vought F4U-4 Corsairs aboard USS *Boxer* (CV-21) operating off Korea in May 1952. It is thought that these Corsairs were assigned to VF-63, although another squadron assigned to the *Boxer* at that time, VF-64, also was equipped with F4U-4s. Both squadrons' Corsairs carried the "M" tail code. In the background are numerous Douglas Skyraiders. *National Museum of Naval Aviation*

An F4U-5, BuNo 121908 and aircraft number 315, assigned to VF-13 has just gone overboard following a failed landing attempt on USS *Wasp* (CV-18) on July 15, 1952. The accident proved fatal to the pilot. *National Museum of Naval Aviation*

Around 1952, two F4U-5s based at Naval Air Station Akron, Ohio, fly over a coastline in the tropics or the subtropics, judging by the numerous palm trees along the shore. Curiously, these planes have the same flame shields and extended exhausts as the F4U-5N night fighters, yet the closer Corsair is marked with BuNo 122033, which was a number issued specifically to an F4U-5, not an F4U-5N.
National Museum of Naval Aviation

A French F4U-7 is parked at a remote air base in mountainous country. This Corsair was assigned at that time to 17 *Flottille*, and bore the fuselage code 17.F.6. The dome of the propeller hub was red. The rudder was painted, front to rear, blue, white, and red, with a black anchor, while the roundel was, from the center out, blue, white, and red, with a thin yellow border and a black anchor.
National Museum of Naval Aviation

An F4U-7 of the French Navy is seen speeding along during takeoff from the flight deck of an aircraft carrier around 1952. The fuselage code is 14F.19, "14F" indicating the plane was assigned to 14 *Flottille*. In French naval aviation, a *Flottille* was an operational squadron. *National Museum of Naval Aviation*

Bombed-up Vought AU-1s of Marine Attack Squadron 212 (VMA-212) are lined up, ready for the next strike mission, at a base in Korea around 1952. The long, white lines with arrows at the front ends were a characteristic marking on that unit's Corsairs at that time. During the Korean war, VMA-212 adopted the nickname "Devil Cats." Later on, the squadron adopted a new moniker, "Lancers." *National Museum of Naval Aviation*

Vought AU-1 BuNo 133843 was photographed in Korea around 1952, while serving with VMA-212. An indistinct inscription, what appears to be a nickname ("MISS"?), is on the cowling. There is an interruption in the straight white line terminating in an arrow, on the forward fuselage and cowling, that may have been the result of a replacement cowling flap. *National Museum of Naval Aviation*

Marine Attack Squadron 212 (VMA-212) was one of the squadrons supplied with the new AU-1 Corsairs in 1952. "JODY" is the nickname painted on the cowling of this AU-1, BuNo 129417 serving with VMA-212 at Pohang Airfield, Republic of Korea, around 1952–53. Note the arrow painted on the cowling.
National Museum of Naval Aviation

The commanding officer of Marine Attack Squadron 324 (VMA-324) shakes hands with a French Navy officer after that squadron delivered a consignment of AU-1 Corsairs, including the one seen here, to the French at Tourane Airfield, Indo-China (later, DaNang, Republic of Vietnam) on April 18, 1954. The carrier USS *Saipan* (CVL-48) transported the AU-1s there. *Naval History and Heritage Command*

In a photograph dated June 19, 1954, these F4U-5s assigned to Naval Air Reserve Training Unit (NARTU) Memphis are equipped with extended exhausts of the type normally associated with the F4U-5N night-fighters. At least the first two Corsairs have blade-type antennas on their turtledecks. The closest plane has the number 3 on the forward main landing-gear doors, while the next three planes lack these doors. *National Museum of Naval Aviation*

F4U-7 BuNo 133727 is shown during an over-water flight while serving with 12 *Flottille* around 1954. The white shape on the vertical fin is an outline of the 12 *Flottille* insignia: a representation of a duck dressed in a naval uniform carrying a blunderbuss against its shoulder. *National Museum of Naval Aviation*

Vought AU-1 BuNo 133842, assigned to the Naval Air Reserve and based at Naval Air Station Minneapolis, Minnesota, is parked with wings folded on a snowy day in 1955. Note the small, round insignia on the side of the turtledeck just aft of the sliding canopy. The interrupted band around the aft part of the fuselage was Orange. *National Museum of Naval Aviation*

Marked "QUANTICO" on its vertical tail, Vought AU-1 BuNo 129411, was photographed on a tarmac at Naval Air Station Glenview, Illinois, in 1956. During that year, the camouflage schemes of USN and USMC Corsairs and other aircraft had been changed from overall glossy Sea Blue to a two-color scheme of Gull Gray over Insignia White, with the latter color also on the rudder and the tops of the control surfaces. *National Museum of Naval Aviation*

The same Vought AU-1 Corsair seen in the preceding photo, BuNo 129411, is viewed from the front right at NAS Glenview in 1956. The number 411 appears on the cowling as well as the forward main-gear doors. The main-gear wheels are a solid-spoked type, painted in an aluminum color. *National Museum of Naval Aviation*